This coloring book belongs to

____

____

____

PHiilelad Ralllian

Afvalgioeo PHLrd Hiison

RLLLD

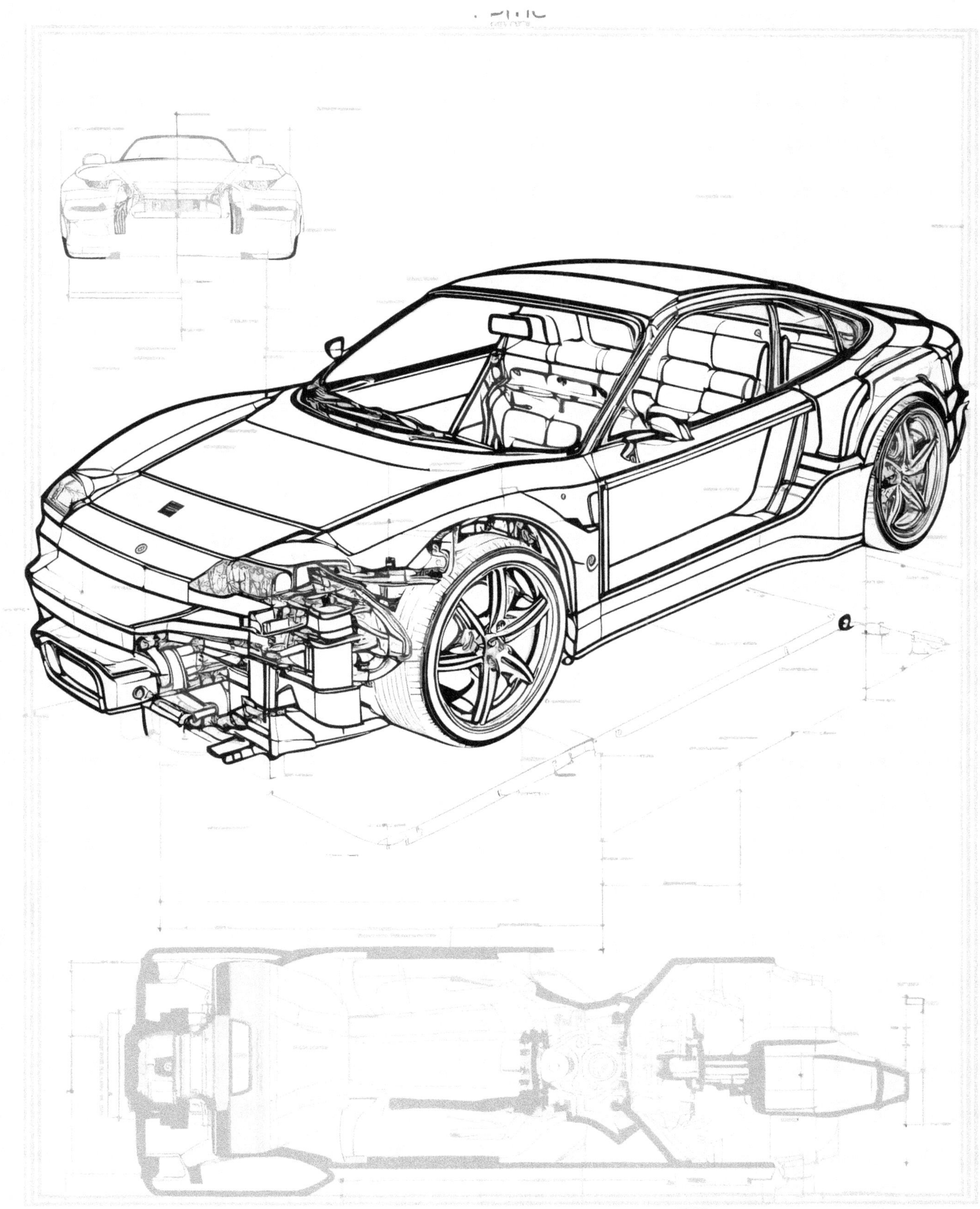

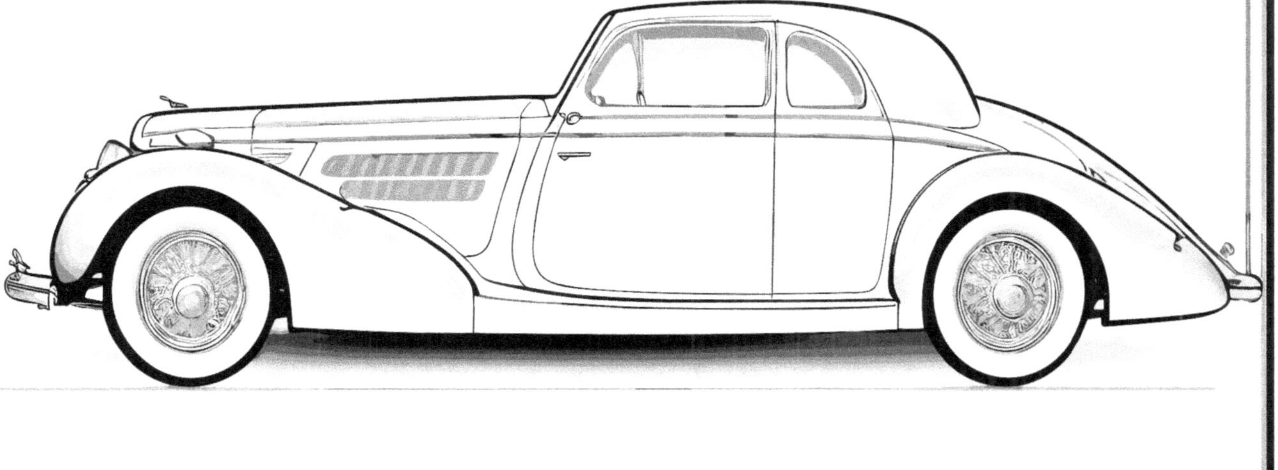

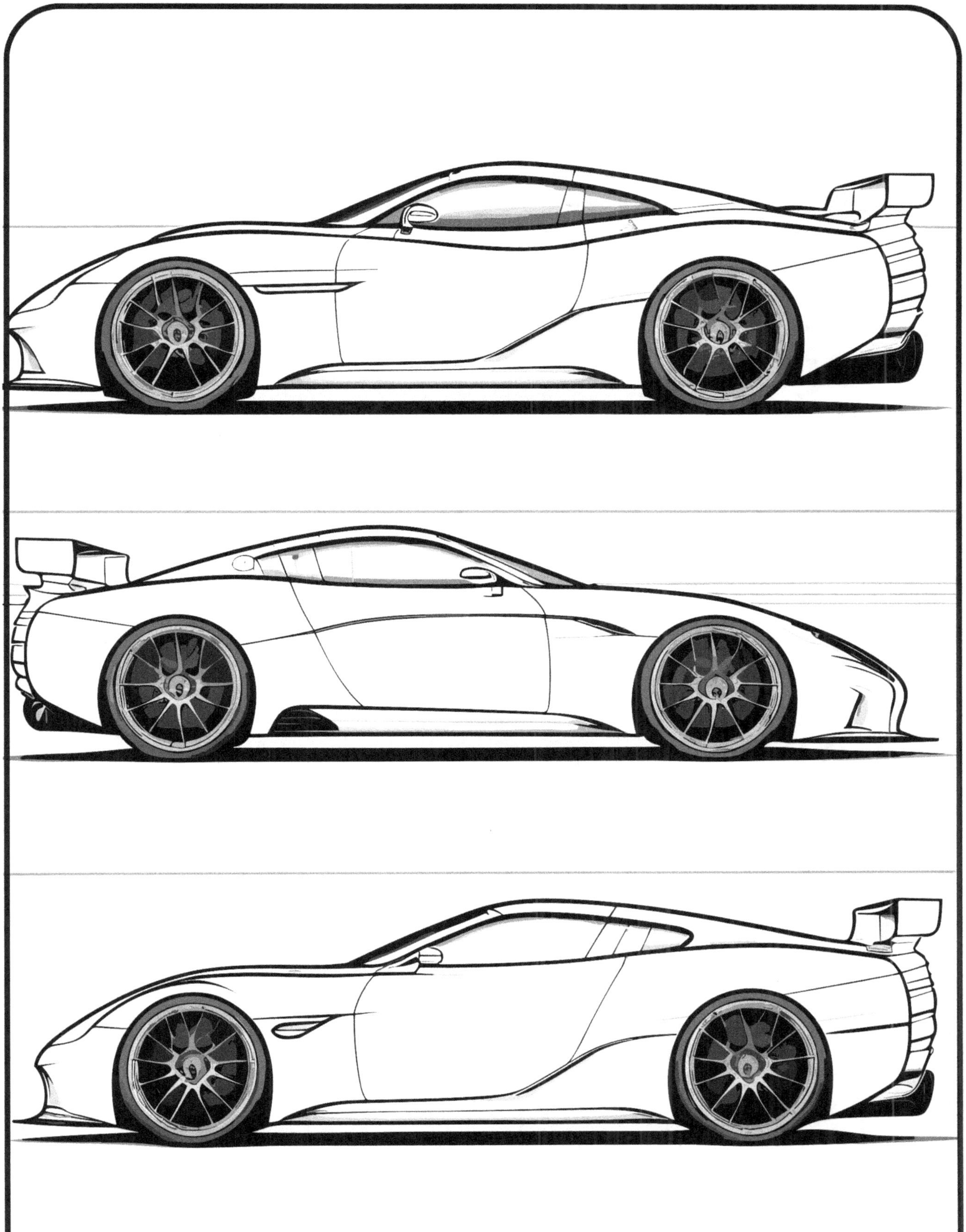

www.ingramcontent.com/pod-product-compliance
Lightning Source LLC
Chambersburg PA
CBHW082150290526
45794CB00008B/3243
* 9 7 9 8 8 5 1 0 5 0 1 9 0 *